Look, We Can Fly Too!

Written by Leya Roberts

Illustrated by Robert Frank

STECK-VAUGHN
C O M P A N Y

A Division of Harcourt Brace & Company

Ronny Raccoon and Manny Moose stood near the woods. They watched Gabby Goose fly over them in the sky. "Wouldn't it be fun to fly?" asked Manny Moose.

"That would be good," said Ronny.

Ronny and Manny stood near the brook. They watched Gabby fly over them in the sky. "Just look at her go!" said Manny.

"I'd like to fly," said Ronny.

Ronny and Manny stood in the meadow. Gabby zoomed by again. "Everything must look better from the sky," said Manny.

"I wish I could fly," said Ronny.

"Gabby, we want to fly too!" cried Manny and Ronny.

"Are you sure?" asked Gabby. "Flying is not for everyone."

"We're sure!" said Manny and Ronny.

"You don't have wings," said Gabby. "If you want to fly, you can use a balloon."

Gabby took out a book about balloons. Then she took out her tool box. They all worked from noon till the moon was high. Soon the balloon was ready to fly.

7

After a good night's sleep, they were
ready to go. Manny, Ronny, and Gabby
climbed into the balloon basket. Up went the
balloon into the sky. "Look, we can fly too!"
said Manny and Ronny.

"Look, Manny!" said Gabby. "Look at the woods down below!"

"Yipes!" said Manny. "This is very scary!" He covered his eyes with his hooves.

"Look, Ronny!" said Gabby. "Look at the brook down below!"

"Help!" said Ronny. "Everything is so very far away!" He hid behind Manny.

"I don't feel so good," said Manny,
holding his head.

"I feel sick too," said Ronny, holding
his tummy.

Gabby let the balloon float down. Soon the balloon was on the ground. Manny climbed out of the balloon basket. He felt very weak and woozy.

Ronny crawled out of the balloon basket and lay down on the ground. "Everything is spinning around and around," he said.

"Gabby, thanks for the balloon ride," said Ronny. "I learned something."

"I learned something too," said Manny.

"What was that?" said Gabby.

"Flying is for the birds!" said Manny and Ronny.

Manny Moose and Ronny Raccoon went right back to the woods. Gabby Goose flew over them.

This time Manny Moose and Ronny Raccoon just smiled and waved.

16